BETTER MAGIC

This is a book that offers
generating ideas.

However, rather than describing brainstorming
processes that already exist, I look to the unconscious
as a source of inspiration.

You already carry this unconscious material with you,
all the time, as a repository, a library of information
inside yourself.

The trick is to use your awareness in order to make
it manifest.

From paper, to objects, to process – my book details
a series of exercises that you can use to build a
relationship with this unconscious element.

To assist me, I call on the influences of art, psychology,
experimental writing, anthropology and concrete poetry.

Always with the intention of waking you up, overturning
conventional processes and finding the best, most
innovative ideas.

It's a journey to the self.

Take a deep breath.

BETTER MAGIC

How to have creative ideas in 24 steps

A TOOLKIT FOR INSPIRATION

MICHAEL ATAVAR

Kiosk
PUBLISHING

info@better-magic.com
www.better-magic.com

ISBN 978-0-9531073-4-6
A catalogue record for this book is available from the British Library.

Artwork by Richard Scarborough
Typeset in Trade Gothic

Praesagans Mens

The unconscious is the real magic of creativity.

CONTENTS

INTRODUCTION

PAPER

OBJECTS

INTRODUCTION

I'm interested in your unconscious, the part of the mind that is not active in waking life, the portion that often only emerges in dreams.

I believe that it can provide you with a limitless source of ideas.

You are carrying with you, all the time, solutions to your creative problems, locked in your head, ready to be accessed.

This book looks at different techniques for uncovering these ideas, always with the intention of bringing this unconscious material into your waking life, your working environment.

If you can get into regular dialogue with this hidden element, you can develop your creative potential.

You simply need to trust your intuition and realise that the solutions that you so ardently seek outside yourself are actually all the time sitting inside you, waiting to be discovered.

So don't be afraid; look forward.

Simply search inside yourself and have a conversation with that part of you that is innately creative.

It knows exactly what to do.

Don't be afraid.

BABER
BABER
BABER
BABER
BABER
BABER
BABER
BABER
BABER
BABER
BABER
BABER
PAPER

WORKING WITH PAPER

This section is about working with paper.

All the exercises and tips in this part of the book encourage you to work with a notepad and pen, remaking words on the page.

This is the basic material of ideas generation. Everyone has a sheet of paper, so begin here with the most primitive of materials.

Remember that developing new ideas is not about expensive tools or the latest technology but about your direct relationship with the page.

In fact, the A4 piece of paper is a perfect vehicle for activating this idea.

Try folding it in half, making a concertina or sticking it together with other pages to form a large map.

The possibilities are endless.

It's the simple power of making that you are cultivating in this section – games on the page that you haven't played since you were a child.

All of this can be achieved by working with paper.

Everyone has a sheet of paper, so begin here with the most primitive of materials.

1 WRITE IT DOWN

- Write down everything that you see.

- Note your thoughts, each one, on the page.

- Trust that wherever you begin is the right place to start.

WRITE IT DOWN

As you read the book, write your ideas down.

It seems obvious. However, in most cases people don't do this, so the concepts escape. They can't remember the exact version of words that made their thoughts so unique.

Ideas have a fleeting life. Writing concretises them on the page, makes them real. It gives them substance.

If you don't download your ideas from your brain to the page on a regular basis, you clog up your mind with old thoughts, now past their sell-by date, and therefore don't create a space for new ideas to come through.

So buy a cheap notepad and pen and write all your ideas down. Every time you have a thought about creativity, your business, products or the client – make a note of it.

Even if you work visually, still write your ideas down.

If the blank page looks empty and frightening, start at the end of your notepad and work backwards, as if you are filling in void spaces, like colouring in a drawing in a child's picture book. Each day complete only a single sheet of paper.

Stalk your big idea slowly. When the notepad is full, your project will be complete.

Ideas have a fleeting life. Writing concretises them on the page, makes them real.

2 | READ DOWN THE PAGE

- Read vertically down the page.

- Find hidden ideas in your text.

- Use these surprising pieces of information to integrate into your ongoing creativity.

READ DOWN THE PAGE

Once you have some words on the page, you can process them in different ways.

The Exercise

Read vertically down the page, using the first or last words of each line to build a new sentence, thereby making something that cuts across conventional meaning.

When I try it now with what I've just written here, I discover –

Making
Meaning
When
Discover

Of course, this doesn't immediately make sense.

However, I might use it as the start of a process, as an instruction – to find new meanings.

It's good information.

Attempt the exercise now with some words that you have written in your notepad.

What do you find?

Don't worry if it's not coherent, if it's a series of titles or descriptions.

All notepads are like this.

Even the most creative people have jotters full of scribbles and lists. Don't worry if it's not instantly recognisable as something serious.

You are always working with small pieces of things.

Perhaps all these scraps, joined together over time, are really the big idea that you have always been looking for?

Don't worry if it doesn't make sense.

WORDS ARE CLUES

It's easy at this stage to give up.

After all, the techniques that I am describing here seldom offer immediate solutions. They require further work from you. Often it's difficult to imagine that any ideas will emerge from these methods.

But they do; I can attest to that.

Words are clues, a trail of breadcrumbs on the page – follow them.

Sometimes what emerges in your notepad might appear off-hand or strange; however, don't reject your outputs as being too outré, too provocative.

Try not to push anything away. Stay with the difficulty and see where it takes you.

The Exercise

Sleep with your notepad under your pillow at night.

Use this night-time technique as a way of focusing your mind on the words on the page.

Is there an idea that can be processed by your unconscious at night, a sentence that can emerge in the daylight, as something new?

Stay with the difficulty and see where it takes you.

3 EMPLOY AMBIGUITY

- Be alert to any double meanings in your text.

- Playfully use these to point you in a new direction.

- Allow the words to open up a new space in your imagination.

EMPLOY AMBIGUITY

Carry your notepad with you at all times and write things down.

I find it useful to mix elements on the page.

A notepad might include –

- Lists.
- Foreign names.
- Diagrams.
- Addresses.
- Ideas.
- Doodles.
- Appointment times.
- Numbers.

Even though your finished page of text might be made up of fragmented, disparate parts, it's actually all you, a reflection of your current creativity, and therefore useful material.

The occasional elisions between these disparate elements on the page are often where new ideas can be found, in the slashes, the confusion.

The Exercise

One way of exploring this ambiguity in your notepad is to read the end of one paragraph, followed by the start of another, as if it were one sentence.

(Even if these texts were written at different times and about opposite subjects.)

This method often creates a third meaning that is unique.

Here are some examples from my own notepad –

- (Making) the sun.
- (Be secret) something.
- (On the street) qualities emerge.
- (Your feet) lightning.

These can lead you in a different direction, one that you couldn't predict before – a completely new territory of 'feet lightning' (whatever that means).

Through this method, you are making physical improvisations with the page, using your own texts as found material.

Try it and see.

Top Tip
If you'd like to take this further, think about using your feet, physicalising these found elements.

If you had to act out 'feet lightning', what would you do?

Get on your feet and see.

Make physical improvisations with the page, using your own texts as found material.

4 | INTEGRATE MISTAKES

- Allow your errors.

- Don't push them away too quickly.

- Use your mistakes to develop unusual product names – brands that other people haven't thought of yet.

INTEGRATE MISTAKES

One method that I use for generating creativity I call 'transition error'.

I write most of my ideas in a notepad, physically inscribing them onto the page. However, when I transfer those notes onto the computer, I often find my handwriting so scrappy or blurred that I have to guess at the words I've written, even if this doesn't at first quite make sense.

These transitions sometimes create new ideas, ones that I wouldn't have considered before.

I find it useful to have several formats on the go and not to dedicate myself to one particular model.

This plurality of devices –

- Loose paper
- Computer
- Cigarette packet
- Notepad
- Restaurant placemat
- Electronic text
- Bus ticket

will encourage some slips and errors to be made, as I slide from one format to the other.

Also, if I'm writing on the computer and I make a very simple error, for example the word 'top' instead of 'too', which is easy to do on the Qwerty keyboard, I always keep this mistake, at least for a few minutes, to see what happens in the sentence, using the original error rather than my intended word.

I incorporate the mistake into my work and see where it takes me.

In the world that we live in, where most product names and processes are already branded and owned, these elisions, the transition errors, are often the only way of thinking of new words, ones that are not yet in the public domain.

Misheard or misspelled words are often useful for product names.

Here is a list of all the errors made in the original draft of this book – grammar, punctuation and misspelling.

It acts as a revue of some of the failed and/or lost ideas in this book.

- IgnmoUse.
- A increased.
- Forzen.
- Soperhaps.

I think of these as potential future projects.

Top Tip
Most of the substance of these errors is nonsense.

But don't be afraid of the nonsensical.

Nonsense is good for undermining the hardwiring of the brain; the eternal search in our mind for habit, conservatism, pattern and repetition.

Errors detonate our expectations, undercutting reason, allowing new connections to briefly take hold.

These errors are the gold of creativity.

Errors are the gold of creativity.

5 | FIND IDEAS IN UNEXPECTED PLACES

- Work outside the office environment.

- With your team, on the move, round the block.

- Avoid gathering for sessions around the familiar conference table.

FIND IDEAS IN UNEXPECTED PLACES

A favourite method of mine for stimulating creativity is to visit an inexpensive Chinese restaurant. Whilst I'm eating my meal, I doodle and write in biro on the disposable paper placemat underneath my bowl.

This is a very contemplative activity; the action of food, of dedication to something else, frees up the mind, so that what I'm noting down (observations, titles, manifestos, ideas) are always secondary to the eating.

This seems to help.

In fact working on two things at once, one of which is physical, often helps creativity come through uninterrupted.

I recently worked on a proposal with a colleague in a busy fast-food sushi restaurant and this environment didn't actually hinder the work. In fact the novelty (neither of us knew the place) positively contributed to the process. Later I sent him a photo of the notes, all scribbled on the paper placemat.

We are often dedicated to working in the office, sometimes in drab rooms, around a table, with no visual or auditory stimulus.

It feels wrong to chop and change the environment.

Yet, in the city, inexpensive solutions to ideas generation are all around us –

- Walks.
- A rowing boat.
- Swimming pools.
- Gardens.
- An escalator.

Take your colleagues out once a week to somewhere unexpected, to signal that things can be different. Choose something that collides with your subject matter, rather than accords with it.

The geographical alteration of space and mood will help you.

Invite them out for a walk, around the block for ten minutes, and brainstorm as you do it. Pull in random observations as you make your tour – a window, a bench, a tree, a roadway.

The Exercise

Perhaps it's the Confucian philosophy, or my use of the *I Ching* in decision making, but I've always found 'Chinese' in a deep part of my creative practice.

I'm reminded that Chinese Whispers are a good way of changing an idea, from something normal to something extraordinary.

Try it this way –

In the group, secretly give one person a product name or description and then let them whisper it to the next person, and so on, until all the circle is complete.

What comes back?

If necessary try this again, feeding the revised name into the system, so in the end a totally transformed word appears.

Use it to generate further process, always shifting your perspectives, to get the best result.

Top Tip
Don't sit around the conference table every time to have ideas.

The table is seniority, investment and solidity, but also inflexibility, routine and boredom.

Take out the table and try the space without the furniture. Even better, if you are feeling adventurous, remove the chairs and sit on the floor.

In this childlike state of remembrance, begin again, reconstructing your creative tasks from the bottom up.

Working on two things at once, one of which is physical, often helps creativity come through uninterrupted.

6 | USE CUT-UPS

- Cut up ten words, then reassemble them on the page.

- Thereby randomising the text.

- Find out the undiscovered feelings behind your words.

USE CUT-UPS

I am influenced by the psychic experiments Brion
Gysin conducted alongside William Burroughs in room
#15 at the Beat Hotel, 9 Rue Gît-le-Cœur, Paris,
during the years 1958-1960.

Gysin created the cut-up technique (a rearrangement
of a text, assembled by chance on the page), then
later the fold-in and faithfully passed the methods on
to Burroughs who used them in subsequent novels,
most successfully in 'Cities Of The Red Night'.

Burroughs and Gysin also stared into mirrors for 24
hours uninterrupted, saw ghosts and made attempts
at time travel. Freed from the world, they could enter
into a limitless psychic reality, outside time and space.

These processes were used to magnetise the
unconscious towards them, using simple techniques
to subvert the real world and convert it to pure
sensation.

I find this fascinating work, completely accurate,
logical and lacking any timidity. Therefore it
encourages in me a kind of fearlessness that is very
useful for working with new ideas; a sense that
everything is possible, that you are a pioneer, that
change is permitted.

(Even if this is not true, positive creativity works like
magic.)

Thus, room #15, 9 Rue Gît-le-Cœur, Paris, has a particular impact on my creativity – even if this is only a fantasy of what really happened.

If I feel devoid of inspiration, I find it useful to project myself there.

In a way, I am doing the same kind of technique of time travel, moving myself back in time, returning to a previous moment of cultural inspiration, for my own enlightenment.

Creativity is nothing other than the audacity to see ghosts, make attempts at time travel, whilst living in a small bedsit room, refusing the limits of the psyche and society and limitlessly projecting yourself into space.

Creativity is nothing but these things.

The Exercise

Take a pair of scissors and cut up a piece of your writing into words and phrases.

Reassemble the disparate parts on a page, paying no attention to their order or form.

(It's always best if you don't think about what you are doing at all.)

Once stuck down, read the adapted text, focusing on any new meanings that have emerged.

Integrate the fragments into your ongoing work. Be bold. Remember the experimental field of room #15.

Integrate Burroughs, find space for Gysin.

Positive
creativity works
like magic.

MAGNETISE AUDACITY

Yourself into space...work...technique...These
processes were...if this is not...the...Burroughs...
limitlessly...9 Rue...outside...of time travel...room
#15...returning to a previous...who used them...
positive...simple...accurate, logical...and lacking
any...of time...and...most successfully in 'Cities'
...is nothing...creativity...to magnetise...audacity...
I find this...Gît-le-Cœur...Even if this is...work...
completely...the cut-up...the psyche...moving myself
back...(Even)...project...Thus, room #15.

A cut-up of the text from the previous page.

In a busy, fast-paced work environment it's often easy
to convince yourself that work with the unconscious
can't be accomplished.

Isn't it impossible?

You feel overwhelmed, pushed for time, working to
deadlines.

However, a cut-up can often give you a few minutes of
space, a reflective moment, within the busyness of the
working day. I find that the cutting up of a client brief
into pieces, the act of remodelling a text, in an
iconoclastic way, is often the physical spur that
changes something inside you.

Try it this way –

The Exercise

Take ten words at random from your client brief and reassemble them on a new page.

If you cheat and try to hold on too closely to what you expect to be revealed, change will be more difficult to achieve – you will simply find out what you already know.

Therefore the chance element is important.

If you believe in the cut-up technique, it will work for you; if you don't expect anything to change, it's unlikely that anything will shift.

After a cut-up, how can you process it?

Often I find that the first phrase pulled out of the hat is a potential title, an overview of the whole piece.

Like 'Yourself Into Space' (found in the cut-up above).

Another method is to look for convergence, a regular repeat of a word or a motif that suddenly leaps out of the fragments. For example, I'm struck by the similarity between the words 'Audacity' and 'Cities' – this gives me a clue that it might be worthwhile to continue to free-associate around the word 'City', in different permutations.

Lastly, try standing up and reading the text out loud. This sometimes transforms what appear to be formless and incoherent words into something bold and emotional.

What is the feeling behind your text?

Deliver your output with some aplomb, to give you an attractive optimism, an audacity that is magnetic to others.

Top Tip
The cut-up often reveals the unconscious intention behind any text. So using this technique, even documents that are factual and dry, like company reports, can suddenly expose hidden elements.

These new cut-up parts can be full of the feelings that were originally denied. So be careful.

In my work, it's often those people who vigorously dispute the presence of feeling who find surprising revelations in these cut-up texts.

Wherever you are, the cut-up will reveal the opposite.

If your company's unofficial policy is to suppress feeling (in 99% of businesses this is the case), then this technique can be a useful method to release built-up tension.

Find out what's really happening in your team by integrating this simple rearrangement of words.

Deliver your output with some aplomb, to give you an attractive optimism, an audacity that is magnetic to others.

CUTTING ROOM FLOOR TECHNIQUE

On my...the limits of...particular impact...used...
into...fascinating...magic...moment...and...magic.

What's left after a cut-up?

Often, the pieces not used can be useful in revealing
a new mood or tone – like a filmmaker who makes a
miniature from the fragments of film that are left on
the cutting room floor.

Here is a diagram of a cut-up from one of my
workshops and the original A4 paper, with the cut-out
parts seen as holes.

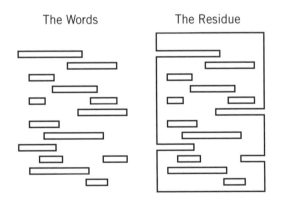

The Words   The Residue

Sometimes, what is left reduces the text to its
essence, a few words that vitally describe the
emotional content of the piece.

In business, we often demand more and more creative resources in order to solve a problem, but sometimes that's just a smokescreen to disguise our own feelings of impotence.

If we can stay with the difficulty (and integrate our own feelings), things can be harder, but more exciting results might emerge.

For example, after your meeting, what remains there, unused on the table?

What are the difficult words left?

Rather than avoiding the feeling, zoom in on its awkwardness.

I find that meetings sometimes escalate, culminating in a brief but forceful exchange of views. Instead, ask for all the conflicting feelings to be present at the start, written down anonymously on sticky cards, arranged on the desk.

Use them as a place to begin.

When I work like this in meetings, there is a collective intake of breath, followed, after five minutes, by relief, when weeks of blocked-up feelings can be looked at and finally integrated.

The following exercise is another way to work with this 'cutting room floor technique'.

The Exercise

Place a large blackboard in your meeting room, over the whole of one surface, and instruct the cleaners in the building not to wipe out what's written there.

In your company brainstorming sessions, always use this blackboard, writing words down in chalk on the surface.

When you enter the room, after another session has taken place, before you erase these texts, look to see if a particular word or title leaps out at you. See if the results of any previous brainstorming can have an impact on your own working process.

Include or integrate any words or titles that you find there.

Rather than
avoiding the
feeling, zoom
in on its
awkwardness.

EXPERIMENTAL CONDITIONS PERSIST

I have hundreds of notepads, all stacked up in the loft, sealed in white plastic boxes

Most of the material remains purely process-based. It's not useful anymore. It simply allows me to keep part of my psyche alive, a sort of repository of experimental me.

It's like a bank vault of ideas, of gold bullion reserves.

However, often I will use notepads from the last year and flick through them, as if they were a cartoon book, giving me brief and succinct impressions of their contents. Occasionally a word will leap out at me which I might fold back into my current process, an older idea reused.

Looking back through my notepads of the last few months, what instantly strikes me is that only a few of these ideas ever find final form, or if they do, it's years before they come to fruition.

Sometimes this might seem like a thankless task.

After all, why work if there are no immediate results, and the outcome is a long way off?

Yet the subtle accumulation of material is always rejuvenating. When you need ideas, material is always there in the background.

Your notepad is a psychic mirror, a place where experimental conditions persist, a space of energetic confluence.

Who is the experimental you?

If you regularly write your ideas down, you automatically help yourself by sharpening your awareness.

You develop your ability to 'see' ideas.

Otherwise you are in a fog, sensing shifts in creativity, but not able to work clearly.

It doesn't matter if the notepad contains doodles, lists or crossings-out. It's a benign space, one that is not focused on outcomes. Everything there can be play, not controlled by the dictates of work, family or colleagues.

The process can be secret.

You don't need to share your ideas-generating methods with anyone. They can remain in your notepad until you decide to divulge them.

This way you can support your own process, piece by piece, slowly discovering what's inside you.

By keeping a notepad you move one step closer to the good idea.

Who is the experimental you?

THE FOLD

This is my version of Brion Gysin's classic fold-in technique.

It's easy, cheap and quick.

If you are working in a creative agency, try this exercise with any documents that you are given, physically manipulating the paper on which the brief is written.

The Exercise

Take a preformatted text and make two parallel vertical folds in the paper.

(It doesn't matter if it's not precise.)

Make a zigzag, folding right to left, creating a text that can be read horizontally, with the missing part hidden by the fold (see the diagram).

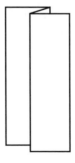

Thus you create all sorts of discontinuities, some of which might be useful for finding a creative solution.

Within the document are all sorts of hidden messages; you are simply piercing the surface to retrieve information locked inside.

According to Gilles Deleuze, French philosopher, the fold is a dynamic space of the self – open to multiple uses and interpretations.

So, fold yourself, fold your organisation.

Top Tip
This method costs nothing. What it does require is perspicacity, commitment to change and a willingness to look at unfamiliar processes.

The adoption of this technique also signals to your team that you, as a leader, are willing to attempt something quite radical. You are prepared to turn things upside down, in search of a more imaginative solution.

Therefore you lead the experiment, with you, as creative leader, at the vanguard.

This requires real audacity.

Creative leadership doesn't come out of benign acceptance of what is; it emerges out of deliberate willingness to experiment with the group.

The Exercise

This is my adaptation of the fold-in, as an instant fold method.

Take a sheet of A4 paper that's already written on and fold it up into quarters. What texts can you see on these four reduced-size pages?

It might not make immediate sense, but trust your first impressions.

Using this technique you have stepped out of what is 'real' into what is 'imagined', 'unreal', 'creative'.

Fold yourself, fold your organisation.

7 | INVITE
NONSENSE

- Don't be afraid of what doesn't make sense.

- Instead, move willingly towards the unconscious.

- Provoke a change in you by building a relationship with the unknown.

INVITE NONSENSE

Usually we are conditioned to avoid nonsense, especially in business where it might be regarded as trivial.

Yet great ideas emerge out of nonsense.

It's only nonsense until, as a brand name, the term becomes absorbed into the mainstream; then it becomes completely legitimised, used by everyone.

One method I use to generate nonsense is an acrostic (a technique where each first letter vertically generates another word horizontally).

You simply complete the blanks with the first thing that comes to mind. However, you need to work fast and accept the first words that come, regardless of their suitability.

For example, if I use 'automatic writing' as the acrostic, I arrive at the following list of words –

All
Upside down
Trees
Over
Matches
And
Tubes
Icicles
Circular

With
Red
Inside
Towns
Inevitably
No one
Gone

This is nonsense.

I'm simply filling in the gaps, as quickly as possible, without any thought to meaning.

However, on my finished list, there are some interesting connections. Especially the first thing that comes out, 'All upside down', a phrase that I might use as an instruction, to integrate into further process.

I might even turn myself physically upside down, do a headstand, to see if I get a better idea.

Why not, if it will provoke a change?

The Exercise

Make an automatic list, using an acrostic, taking time to pick out any interesting terms that emerge.

Do any of these phrases apply, even in the broadest sense, to any business problems that you are currently experiencing?

For example, on my list, the phrase 'over matches' might mean that there's too much agreement in my current practice.

If so, I might think of mismatching some things, to obtain a better result.

Always look out for this ambiguity, these secondary meanings. They are a good sign of what's under the surface of your texts.

Top Tip
It's useful to have someone in your group sessions who can record what's happening and look out for these hidden meanings.

Choose this scribe from the group and rotate the role regularly.

It's almost impossible to lead the group and be alert to these subtle changes.

So give yourself a break.

Did they notice something that you didn't?

Great ideas
emerge out
of nonsense.

THE NOIGANDRES

In my teenage years, I felt the full force of the impact of 1950s Brazilian concrete poetry. The Noigandres group, particularly Augusto de Campos, had an enormous effect on me.

As I look at the article 'Communication And Structure In Concrete Poetry', written by Ian Hamilton Finlay in the magazine 'Image – Kinetic Art, Concrete Poetry', while researching the material for this book, I feel a nostalgic wave for this work, carrying me back to the years of my 1970s.

As a consequence of this continued influence, even now my notepads are full of all sorts of word games.

They include –

- Anagrams.
- Codes.
- Reversed words.
- Acronyms.

These aggregates spill down the page, words criss-crossing in chaotic relationships.

In fact the word 'Noigandres' looks to me just like an anagram.

These word games are like the thin pale strips of paper emerging from shredding machines in the office. They perform a similar function – as padding, fertiliser, insulation, nesting. They are a constant source of new material.

They work by turning over the ground of my creative life, as if prodded by a rake. They don't make things happen but they provide the appropriate conditions from which creative ideas can grow.

For example, the product names 'Sgnuj', 'Què és' and 'Sdrac' were all generated by similar processes.

Top Tip
If you are a team leader with the responsibility of generating ideas, it's useful to have some dedicated physical resources, that you collect, that can be used in your creative sessions.

Toys, material, colour swatches – these are all useful.

In fact you might use these elements as if in a game, mixing and matching pieces: a clash of colours, a combination, a temporary collision.

What magical residues do these provide?

Don't be fearful of apparent 'failure'.

The revolutionary idea is always found in the random, accidental fusion of elements.

The
revolutionary
idea is always
found in the
random,
accidental
fusion of
elements.

8 | TRY WORD GAMES

- Games help you to unlock your blocks.

- Play to release the answer.

- The solution is always available in a simple rearrangement of words.

TRY WORD GAMES

If you are stuck, try to create an anagram of the concept that frustrates you.

So, for example –

- 'Office politics' becomes 'piccolo fifties'.
- 'Brief' becomes 'fibre'.
- 'Deadline' becomes 'ideal den'.

This frees something up, as if the difficulty becomes suddenly detonated.

It makes a game of what was previously a chore, the inevitable routine of delivering, every day, creative responses to challenging client briefs.

Sometimes these word games become simply process – nothing more than play, working on the page, manipulating ideas.

Thus the 'brief' literally becomes 'fibre', an ongoing dialogue with yourself.

If you place yourself in a positive attitude towards your creativity, processing all the time, even when on the move, on a train, or on your underground journey to work, then new ideas are more likely to stick.

The alternative is only to be creative when in brainstorming meetings – this sometimes works, but it's more hit and miss.

Placing yourself regularly in the path of creativity, on an ad hoc basis, is more difficult, but more effective in the long-term.

Top Tip
Ignore creativity at your peril (your competitor won't).

If you only work with what you can see, the definite, the known, the logical, you can survive for a long time, possibly forever, but you will never be a market leader. Companies at the forefront of innovation are working with challenging techniques in order to maintain their market advantage.

They are integrating mystery into their process to generate the indefinable X.

Use this quality yourself by following some of the exercises in this section: scrambling words, running them backwards, turning the text on its head and making acrostics. Have faith in these word games – they will reveal parts of you that previously remained hidden.

The more that you tune in with yourself, the more you will find creativity evident in your own environment.

For example, I recently found a pile of old audio cassettes on the pavement waiting to be taken away; amongst them was a Ludwig van Beethoven tape. On the cover some of the letters had rubbed off, so the name was spelt incorrectly as 'B THOVI-N'.

I immediately considered 'THOVIN' as the title of a possible product.

In this case I didn't have to play a word game, it was done for me – all I had to do was pay attention (and not reject the suggestion out of hand, as some nonsense).

This 'noticing' is at the centre of ideas generation.

If you really open your eyes, everything is already there in front of you.

Make a game of what was previously a chore.

START IN THE WRONG PLACE

My 'associative word technique' is a simple way with words, a psychological staple that always stimulates new ideas.

Try it this way –

The Exercise

Free-associate around any current word.

For example, if I were to start with the word 'difficulty', I might find –

- Difficulty.
- Challenge.
- Quiz.
- Lottery.
- Spark.
- Chain.
- Fence.
- Rapier.
- Cut.
- Z.

When I try this exercise myself, I get stuck around the Z. I freeze up. So this is where I might find the energy of my current blockage.

So I would continue to work with Z, making all sorts of associations with the letter.

I imagine 'Zorro' cutting a series of slashes through the process of difficulty.

The trick is not to overthink the problem and to work as rapidly as possible, not allowing your conscious mind to take over. Don't try and give the response that you think will be expected – the cool, clever reply.

There is no right or wrong in this exercise, just a series of rapid, reflex responses.

Sometimes, when I run this exercise in a group, a random word will jump out of the list. I remember on one occasion, in an advertising agency, when the word 'tractor' suddenly emerged. This was such a shock to the group that we continued to free-associate around this word, using its earthy qualities to turn over the idea, as if we were ploughing, making a rich terrain of the product material.

Top Tip
It actually doesn't matter where you start.

The big fear is that we must begin perfectly and have a good plan.

Yet I believe it's better just to dive in.

This can be in any part of the process – if you can't start in the right place, start in the wrong place. The main thing is to start somewhere.

Lists of words can also be helpful in creating rapid-fire blasts of ideas.

I often find these tables in out-of-date language study books that I buy in second-hand bookshops, then readapt for a new purpose. Many times these old books are free or cost only a few pence each.

Robbed of meaning, these word juxtapositions can often generate new processes.

For example –

A long time...	Not...	Tomorrow...
Now...	Never...	Since...
Even...	Nothing...	Behind...
Less...	No...	In front...
Where...	Isn't...	Still...
Sometimes...	Didn't...	At last...

They are found objects, naturally occurring 'associative word techniques' that can be reappropriated for a different purpose.

Realigning these lists, reading across rather than top to bottom, I create slogans like 'Where Isn't Still' or 'Even Nothing Behind'.

Some of which might help me in my quest for new ideas.

If you can't start in the right place, start in the wrong place.

ENDUCTION

The unconscious can provide you with all sorts of material that's readily available inside you – if you are willing to listen.

Much of this content is useful for generating ideas.

However, you have to understand that solutions are not easy, readily available; they will not automatically arrive.

You need to invite them in.

Process is key – the turning over of notepad material every day to optimise mistakes (errors of typing, confusion, strange collisions).

You have already looked at some of these methods: 'Read Down The Page', 'Employ Ambiguity', 'Integrate Mistakes', 'Use Cut-ups', 'Try Word Games', 'Invite Nonsense'.

The world is full of experimental methodologies.

Yet, as a creative leader, it's necessary to make yourself the site of these experiments, to show that you are capable of putting yourself on the line, in the service of the brief.

The good idea is classless.

The good idea
is classless.

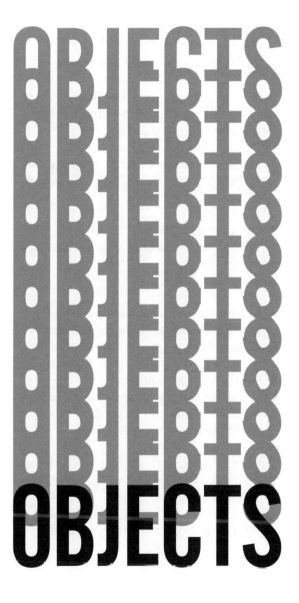

WORKING WITH OBJECTS

This section is about working with objects.

Because they are external to you, you can download your feelings into them and then they can act on your behalf, as transitional objects.

And because objects are you (but not really you), you can be free with how you use them, just like throwing a ball or riding a bicycle.

If you only stay in your head, locked in the problem, it's difficult to move forward. Objects allow you to place these problems in a different space and so see them from the outside.

If you are a team leader, always have lots of physical objects to work with, to challenge and inspire your colleagues.

None of these need be expensive. Use things that cost very little. It's always your creative overturning that you are exploring through these materials, rather than attempting to show off your seniority.

Always expose yourself to process – do it first yourself. Take a personal chance and inspire the people around you to take a small step forward.

All this can be accomplished by using objects.

Take a personal chance and inspire the people around you to take a small step forward.

9

USE
YOUR
HANDS

- Put your hands on something.

- Feel its charge, let it transfer its power to you.

- Touch is the start of your own imaginative journey.

USE YOUR HANDS

Your hands are tactile receptors, highly sensitive
fingers, like an antenna searching out data.

Use them to gather information from the object you
are holding, unconscious impressions that are not
controlled by the logical mind. Your hands unlock
these sense impressions from within an object,
encouraging rapid-fire images to emerge.

Often we are so locked in our mental faculties, trying
desperately to make the ideas fit together like a jigsaw
puzzle, using only text to transmit concepts, that we
disregard a whole area of opportunity – our bodies
and hands.

These sensory devices are with us all the time, yet we
rarely use them.

I believe that there is a transfer of creative energy
from the object to the brain and from your imagination
to the thing, igniting the item itself – a two-way
conversation.

And we can provoke this transfer to stimulate ideas.

For example, if I directed you to leave your desk now,
walk out of the office and find a tree, then place your
hand on any part of its surface face down, palm
extended flat, like a sensory device, a scanner, onto
the tree's bark and close your eyes, I guarantee that a
shock of images would emerge from this contact, an

electric counterpoint to the object you have just touched.

And if you did this every day, on the way to work, to charge yourself up with ideas, like a battery, this would be time well spent.

Don't worry what everyone else is doing, or whether you think it's an absurd idea. Follow your own path. Try it and see.

Objects put us in the way of feelings, things that we'd often rather ignore.

The body brings us back time and time again to reality. The body has its own truth, its own veracity.

Touch is the transfer, the fuse paper, the way in.

Top Tip
Remember that what you touch leaves a charge, an echo, so the more that you can build things with your hands in the creative process, the more you will leave a trail behind you, a mark from your consciousness, on the material.

Avoid the computer and work with your hands instead. Build an object in the real space of a room.

The Exercise

Think about your body. Remain in contact with it all day.

Touch is the
transfer, the
fuse paper,
the way in.

10

FOLLOW THE STREET

- Don't be afraid of rubbish.

- Use what other people discard to your own advantage.

- Innovation always happens on the fringes of culture, where you least expect it.

FOLLOW THE STREET

The Surrealists loomed large in my early life.

Sometimes these chance encounters with Surrealism –
Aragon, Breton, Dalí – provided a rich loam for me,
out of which I could develop and grow.

I was particularly attracted to their idea that
everything could be found on the street – poetically
illustrated in Louis Aragon's 1926 book 'Le Paysan
de Paris'.

In the city, the street is where energy accumulates.

In places like London my eye always goes towards
rubbish, convinced that these abandoned things are
creative. What everyone else discards can be
cherished, brought back to life in an altered form,
and these objects, sheared of their original meaning,
repurposed, can help me to generate ideas.

In my twenties I spent a lot of time sifting through
physical rubbish, looking for ideas. But even now, if
I want to find a new concept, I'm unlikely to sit at
my desk, waiting. If stuck, I wander the streets, eyes
focused on the ground, looking for what the world
throws at me, as if by accident.

Here, on the pavements, nothing is fixed. It's all an
accidental process, where everything can be found,
both physical and psychic.

In every city you can visit the commercial quarters at the weekend and see what's abandoned on the street – shelves, magazines, display units, catalogues.

Many of these can be used in your creativity. You become a unconscious collector, sifting through the debris, remaking it, looking for ideas.

In fact, I often wonder if these random piles of discarded furniture are, in themselves, art objects, ready to be recorded or photographed by the discerning eye.

These thoughts about the street I still use every day, integrating this and other creative techniques into business contexts.

I often send the participants of my workshop to look for objects.

They search in –

- City parks
- Second-hand shops
- Discount supermarkets
- Wastepaper bins

looking for inspiration.

The unconscious of the group, of the work environment, even of the city itself can be discerned from what they find on the street.

For example, a saw from a hardware shop provides them with a clue to cutting through. Or an accidental plastic bag, caught by the breeze, reminds them of adaptability. Even a flower in a shop window puts them in touch again with vulnerability.

All of these feelings can be integrated into their process, challenging them with things they had momentarily forgotten in the business's great push to get ahead.

Thus, the future of the project can sometimes be discerned from what they find on the street.

The Exercise

Go outside now and pick up the first thing that you find.

Even if it's a squashed can of cola, integrate its message in a dynamic, considered way.

Thus, creativity is always available, inviting you to deal with the present, to avoid cliché, to be real.

The crushed metal of the can's compressed logo has a message.

It's the real thing.

Creativity
is always available, inviting us to deal with the present, to avoid cliché, to be real.

PAPER PLANE

Today I found the remains of a cigarette packet on the street, flattened, no brand name visible; it looked just like a paper plane.

I wondered, what does this paper plane mean to me?

When I thought about it, I realised that it was an invocation for me to fly, to soar, so I spent a few thoughtful minutes integrating this idea into my process.

It reminded me that it's always the significance that you assign to these objects that counts.

The small, unknown step between you and it creates a jolt, a gap, and it's in this sudden space that the unconscious briefly emerges.

I quickly take a page of my manuscript and fold it into a paper plane and throw it across the room, evoking a feeling of childhood, of school, both uncontained and oppressive.

When the will is activated in a positive manner, the results are always imaginative, alive, even if dense and complex.

I think for a moment.

Perhaps my creativity could simply be paper folds?

When the will
is activated
in a positive
manner, the
results are
always
imaginative,
alive.

CHINESE TILES

In the boardroom it might be difficult to imagine that the solution to your complex problem could, in fact, be nothing other than this worthless item, a flattened cigarette packet.

Yet, please persist.

Have faith in the process.

I guarantee that there are ideas out there, all around you, just waiting to be found.

I believe that the extension of your will into the world, from the confines of logic to the profound voodoo of the outside, will liberate you and provide you with a good source of creative concepts.

My techniques work because they force you to take a different path from the normal route that you follow to produce ideas – they challenge the deadening effect of habit.

Even within the most radical of business enterprises, routines and shortcuts soon take over.

These methods force you to take the longer, unexpected way round and so frustrate your usual ways of working.

Try the following exercise –

The Exercise

On the way to a meeting, use the street as a resource.

Get out of your car and walk the last ten minutes.

See if you can find three items that connect together to form a whole. These can be inconsequential – a piece of sticky tape, a leaf, a coffee cup.

Now force a connection between two or more of these objects. What's the common thread? When you have this link, see if you can apply it to any aspect of your next meeting.

Does this allow a moment of insight?

Often I try this exercise on the way to a workshop and I'm always astonished by the volume of objects that I see abandoned on the street – sometimes hundreds of items.

On one occasion I found a 'Chinese' tile, a black plastic rectangle that had been smeared with white glue, then thrown on to the street. The patterns formed by this random application were exotic, unknown, exciting.

I picked it up to show to the group, as an example of the unconscious in action.

Force yourself to take the longer, unexpected way round and so frustrate your usual ways of working.

11 | BE PHYSICAL

- Integrate the physical.

- Concretise your processes in order to give them form, stability.

- Deliberately bring the idea back to your body.

BE PHYSICAL

If stuck, physicalise the problem, act it out.

This takes the difficulty out of your head and transcribes it into another form that might help to illuminate the original problem.

For example, literally place a glass against the wall of your building, to sense what's going on inside, to tune into your company's philosophy from the outside, to sense what's coming in the future.

Use this mediumistic technique, this obverse approach, to obtain real clarity.

Like a trapper of old, sense the energy of the ground, of the land, to hear the rumbles, the creativity, the voids, the inspiration, the space between.

Integrate it into your process to challenge the logic of easy solutions.

Your body is the answer. Use yourself as the magic, the object, the amplifier.

Also, by doing this, by evoking the maverick, the surreal, the active, you place yourself outside habit, in a place of embarrassment, ready to receive what the universe might unexpectedly offer you.

For example –

- Stand on a chair to get an overview of the problem.
- Turn your back to your desk to approach the challenge from the reverse.
- Switch the light switch on and off in a room to illuminate difficulty.
- Lie on the floor to get another angle on your situation.

(These are just some of my suggestions.)

When you are blocked, uninspired, you are usually stuck in your head, whilst your body can remain free, so it's useful to involve yourself physically in the active solution.

Your body can solve the problem for you.

Sometimes organisations won't integrate these techniques because they are too eccentric, or perhaps because they don't want to move away from the comfort of an entrenched position.

However, if unacknowledged by the business, these problems will go underground, into the collective psyche of the company and create a perpetual stalemate that will stymie creativity.

The only way to challenge the situation is to act it out physically.

Top Tip

In a recent workshop I talked about colour as a method for stimulating ideas.

One participant asked me 'Do you mean that if I stand next to a pink car, I might get a better idea?'

It was exactly right.

If you physicalise your abstract thoughts, you have a better chance of working with them. Otherwise they stay in your head and don't move.

Like the example of the pink car, you direct yourself on a physical journey and so activate a part of yourself that is creative.

Your body can solve the problem for you.

SIXTY SECONDS

Sometimes the simplest solutions are the most difficult for us to try – their very simplicity challenges us to use ourselves in a direct, uncomplicated way.

For example, if we are reduced to one sense, to merely seeing, what happens?

The Exercise

Look at any object for sixty seconds.

Make a written list of the qualities that you notice – tone, colour, texture,

Remember to push yourself, to keep going. If you can't immediately see anything, look again. Your best work will come when you are at your most empty, scrambling around for images and impressions to fill the void.

Don't worry – something will come.

But you must persist.

Take some time to search beyond the obvious.

I'm aware that this is the opposite approach to the usual methods of brainstorming, where background knowledge is prioritised and data research is key.

However, I say, ignore the seduction of data.

Try the unconscious in sixty-second bursts only.

Top Tip
Another way of having ideas is to work fast.

If you work quickly, as if on automatic, not thinking too much about what you are doing, the unconscious has a chance to survive. If you deliberate, your ego takes over and smoothes out all the possible idiosyncrasies.

Try these 'Ten Rules For Finding A Creative Solution' –

- Use a colour.
- Spend less than £20.
- The title is a made-up name.
- Include a five-word slogan.
- The solution must be less than one page of A4.
- Complete in under 15 minutes.
- Invent a customer.
- Draw the product on paper.
- Work in reverse order.
- Add a feeling word.

If I ask you to find a solution, I want you to use your first impulse, your unmediated response.

Go instantly to the first object that you find, whether it's screwed-up paper, a mirror or a wristwatch, and build a relationship with that object.

The first thing that you discover becomes the solution (the mirror might suggest some 'reflection' that is the answer to the problem).

I like this way of working a lot. It makes things very easy. By limiting your creative choices to what's around you, you are forced to suddenly confront a decision, cutting through layers of obfuscation.

It's also possible to work with this technique in a group context –

The Exercise

Split your colleagues into teams of two or three.

Set a creative brief, with a solution time of ten minutes. Time it accurately. Only allow what is in the room – either externally (chairs, table, curtains, windows) or in the bags of the participants (magazines, paper, mirrors, pens etc.).

Force people to work with the slightest means possible. Disallow any digital materials that offer a wider window into other opportunities.

Remember you are reducing options.

Insist on a performed solution.

Try the
unconscious
in sixty-second
bursts only.

NO ACCIDENTS

If I am trying to think of a creative solution, I look around me and use whatever is to hand, however incongruous it first appears.

I trust that my unconscious has selected this item for me, offering me a simple solution, which is not actually instant at all, but filtered in complicated ways through the brain's retrieval systems.

Therefore, I don't believe in the accidental any more – it's merely a manifestation of the mind's sophisticated processing, presented as chance.

However, you don't need to have any philosophical position on this, you can simply trust what turns up.

A good example of this is my last book, 'Everyone Is Creative'.

During the production process I went through many choices of colour for the cover, until at last I used the green from the back of an old Simca car manual (that I had picked up for free), which just happened to be on my desk when I had to make my final decision.

After a year's deliberation, the first thing that came to hand became the solution.

The Exercise

Assign your team members the task of bringing to the meeting a number of objects that attract them.

(These could be found in the office, on their desk, in the storeroom.)

Once all the objects have arrived, ask the group to individually arrange all the disparate pieces into a construction that makes some sense to them – colour, volume, concept.

The structuring that each person uses always tells an individual story.

- In a line.
- Conflicting objects.
- On top of each other.
- Using a reduced number.
- In a pyramid.
- Colour coded.
- Remade as a map.

Take some time to process the results. Often these simple constructions can be integrated in a very direct way into your product development or output schedule.

In one session that I ran, the group members were each given the instruction to bring five items to the workshop.

They selected –

- Peanut.
- Hook.
- Die.
- Envelope.
- Snap fastening.
- Curve.
- Seal.
- Lemon.
- Coffee grinder.
- Doll's Alpine hat.
- Sticky tape.
- Paintbrush.
- Insect repellent.
- Holy water.
- Twig.
- Matches.
- Scissors.
- Ashtray.
- Book.
- Snorkel.
- Diary.
- Felt-tip pen.
- Inkwell.
- Spoon.
- Güiro.

Out of these chaotic items, they each imposed order, eloquently stating something revealing about the group dynamic.

The first thing that comes to hand becomes the solution.

12 | PROVOKE BAD IDEAS

- Put your bad ideas on the table first.

- Use this method to encourage all members of your team to have a voice.

- Even bad ideas can be a vehicle for transformation.

PROVOKE BAD IDEAS

Exposure is rich in creative potential.

If we don't reveal things about ourselves, nothing that we make has anything individual about it, anything unique.

Sometimes embarrassment helps us have new ideas.

One way of working with this idea of exposure is to rapidly reveal things at the start of any creative session, thereby allowing everyone in the group to have a voice.

I suggest the following exercise –

The Exercise

In a brainstorming session, immediately put all the bad ideas on the table first.

Anything that you find –

- Stupid.
- Obvious.
- Inappropriate.
- Ridiculous.
- Negative.

A clichéd slogan, a terrible image.

Put as many of these on the table as quickly possible – twenty, thirty, forty. This throws out all the surface froth of the imagination, the things that you feel but daren't say, and therefore allows different concepts to emerge.

Sometimes, even these 'bad' ideas are quite good.

Someone in the group is holding back on a thought that might be useful, for fear of ridicule.

Yet it might be good.

Or within the forty 'bad' ideas an interesting collision might emerge that reveals something new, some maverick suggestion that takes you beyond the limits previously imposed.

Also, this exercise is about being seen.

It employs a democratising technique, in order to allow everyone in the session to be visible, even for a few seconds.

In that blink of an eye, the unconscious can reveal itself and allow all sorts of interesting material to burst out.

Don't ignore the 'bad' ideas – there is enormous volume in this erratic substance.

Top Tip

Draw a vertical line down a sheet of A4 paper. On the left hand side title the list 'Bad Ideas', on the right 'Good Ideas'.

Bad Ideas	Good Ideas

Write twenty first thoughts in each column, as quickly as you can. Then read across in rows, from left to right, across the 'bad' and 'good', merging the two.

Are there any useful crossovers?

Exposure is rich in creative potential.

13 | REMEMBER THE ANONYMOUS

- Any object can be a conduit for creativity.

- Even the things that you find on the street.

- The more incongruous the better, giving space for you to explore reality without limits.

REMEMBER THE ANONYMOUS

I use the 'random book technique' a lot in my work.
I open a book at any page and look at the first thing
that attracts my eye.

It's not important what the book is, or how you come
by it – choose any volume. Simply open it at random
and pick out the first sentence that you see. Try to
make a connection with the words on the page and
stick with the feeling, even if it's not immediately
clear what it signifies.

What's your first impression, your instinctive reaction?

The words that you choose might allow you to tune
into something that's inside you, something from
which you're unconsciously trying to protect yourself.

Another of my twists on the 'random book technique'
is that I go into railway station bookshops and repeat
the process, using any paperback that I find on the
shelves.

It doesn't really matter what I choose, even the latest
blockbuster will do, because I am simply trying to
make a connection with my own unconscious material,
through the medium of the text.

The anonymous setting of a railway station is just
right, the perfect blank canvas for this kind of
exploration.

In stations or airports, the pace is so rapid and so relentless that I don't really think about what I am doing, so my mind switches off, I am busy with other things, and I can more easily assimilate new ideas.

The barriers that I build up around me, that protect me from change, can collapse here, across the time zones, one piece at a time.

When I travel I always keep a pen in my hand, ready to make notes should a concept arise.

The airport helps my ideas 'take off'.

The Exercise

Send out members of your team to magazine shops, the news stand, the bookshop or the railway station and instruct them to find some printed material, the first thing that they see.

Come back and process it as a group. Use the results to impact on your new idea.

Adrift.
I just live in these parts, I told him.
Why have you come?
Intermittently.
Quite sure.

(Five things that I found today at random from books.)

If your mind switches off, if you are busy with other things, you can more easily assimilate new ideas.

14

INTEGRATE THE REVERSE

- Walk in reverse.

- Attempt to do two things at the same time.

- In the white noise of inverted expressions, find new and original ideas for creativity.

INTEGRATE THE REVERSE

'Reverse steps' is a physical technique that I've developed to help unlock the brainstorming process.

It's the conjunction of two things – thinking forwards and moving backwards. Since one process is forward acting (thinking) and one action is physically in reverse (walking), the mixture of the two can provide some surprising results.

Try it this way –

The Exercise

Think of a challenge that you are currently experiencing. Perhaps it's a work problem, a creative block or a new brief.

Hold it in your mind's eye.

Stand up, looking forwards with your eyes open, then slowly, very carefully, walk backwards. At the same time free-associate on the subject of your problem, making a series of random word associations.

Often, it's useful to do this in pairs, so that another colleague can help you. The other person simply watches you through the entire process and physically supports you.

Perhaps you are you are thinking of a new type of carbonated drink, so you might come up with –

- Drink.
- Brink.
- Cliff.
- Beach.
- Pirates.
- Riches.
- Treasure.
- Gold.

Take your time.

Once your list of words is complete, reflect on the material that emerged.

For example, in the list above, the words might give me an idea of colour 'Gold' or feeling 'Cliff', meaning precipice, a rollercoaster of emotions that might be useful for a fizzy drink.

Trust your first impressions.

Often, when you run the exercise a second time, you will have already become adept at sidestepping your unconscious, able to avoid any embarrassment.

Be careful. Ideas come through visibility. Your first awkward, unformed feedback will be the most helpful.

Cherish these valuable mistakes.

Top Tip

Or try reversing yourself. Adopt some awkward pose, a body adaptation that makes it difficult to think straightforwardly.

Free-associate whilst you –

- Shake hands with yourself.
- Brush your hair in a mirror.
- Look backwards, over your shoulder.
- Stand up and sit several times in a row.
- Turn a radio slowly on and off.
- Click your fingers.

(Balancing a hardback on your head is also good.)

Try reversing
yourself.

INVERTED CONSTABLE

I integrated the 'inverted constable technique' after
a visit to the Fundació Pilar i Joan Miró (Joan Miró
Museum) in Mallorca.

On one canvas I saw, Miró had taken a shop-bought,
cheaply framed reproduction of 'The Haywain', turned
it upside down and painted on the surface, using his
own distinctive figures.

It reminded me that even classics, turned upside
down, can have something new to say.

Recently, I used an upside down Constable painting,
'Flatford Mill (Scene On A Navigable River)', as an
example in a workshop, making a large multi-sheet
version and inviting the participants to draw on it,
adding their observations, updating the painting in
a modern, iconoclastic way.

They each saw shapes, people, structures, objects.

Turned upside down, the painting was able to reveal
its unconscious side. It stopped being 'Flatford Mill'
and turned into a much more modern representation
'Scene On A Navigable River'.

It reminded me that the solution is already in our
hands – it just needs to be reversed in order to reveal
its inner meaning.

Even classics, turned upside down, can have something new to say.

PRINTING UPSIDE DOWN

In a busy fast-paced work environment, it often feels difficult to dedicate time to these unconscious experiments.

The following exercise allows you to integrate the accidental, the maverick, through a simple physical process.

When I was writing this book, I ran out of paper so I had to print the new document on the reverse of an older manuscript. When I saw the printed pages, I was shocked at some of the relationships that emerged between the front and back of my A4 sheets.

I had even accidentally overprinted some texts and I noticed that a few key words leapt out, alerting me to ideas that I had forgotten about –

- 'Anti-textual.'
- 'Avoid the head.'
- 'Looking.'
- 'Chaos is OK.'
- 'Permission.'

So I wove these phrases into the updated manuscript.

The Exercise

Keep your old A4 throw-away paper in a box.

This can be any sort of material that's not needed any more – accounts, old client proposals, colour diagrams.

Print out your new creative documents using this recycled paper.

Afterwards, look at the relationship between what you have just printed and the material on the reverse. Sometimes sympathies emerge between the two sides of the paper.

You can integrate this technique in two ways –

Before your brainstorming meeting, print the latest client brief onto the reverse sheets of the recycled paper. Don't try and rig these 'accidents'. Simply take the pages off the top of the recycle pile and feed them into the printer.

Once the document is assembled, is there anything that attracts your attention?

Is there a question from the brief (front) that the reverse (back) can answer?

Avoid the head and work instinctively.

Secondly, if you are a creative leader, always have a pile of these recycled pages to hand. If you become stuck, randomly introduce some of these verso sheets into your ongoing teamwork.

This requires some nerve – you must be confident enough with your team to be seen to fail.

Have the self-possession to integrate the unexpected.

Top Tip
The reverse can easily be adapted into a simple word game.

Take some terms from the client's brief – a concept, a tag line, a location – and reverse the text.

So –

- Travel = Levart.
- Sales = Selas.
- Office = Eciffo.

Use these as titles in your work, parts of new texts or as the names of objects that you are designing. Often these reversals look like vocabulary from a Polynesian language or products from a Swedish DIY superstore.

Momentarily shift your perspective from the everyday to the poetic.

Shift your perspective from the everyday to the poetic.

15 | WORK BACKWARDS

- Walk and talk backwards.

- Use this method to evoke a temporary dream experience.

- Play with the idea of backwards – on the street, in a train, waiting for a plane.

WORK BACKWARDS

One technique that I have found useful in waking up
my unconscious is working backwards.

If you can make something move in reverse, then new
ideas will emerge. The technique works for anything –
a word, a sound, a narrative, a photograph.

During the process of turning it backwards, something
gets revealed that you couldn't see before –

- A shape.
- A waveform.
- A texture.
- A meaning.

Flip, invert, reverse, turn upside down.

This method is like magic; one minute a word is there,
solid, and the next moment it gets transformed into
something else liquid, enigmatic.

I recently went to see Salvador Dalí's house in Port
Lligat, Cadaqués. During the visit, I viewed some films
that Dalí had made where he reversed the direction
of the celluloid, giving the impression that he was
pouring water or throwing a ball backwards. Simple
acts of modern sorcery.

The same kind of tricks that I had once witnessed in
Jean Cocteau's film 'Orphée', magical revisions of the
normal world.

It reminded me that the use of this 'backwards technique' shows our willingness to be ourselves in reverse, to transform, to play.

I wonder what it would be like if we turned the whole world 'backwards' and looked at everything as though it were flexible, malleable – simple, fluid material, open to change?

Try it and see.

Integrate backwards working to change the future.

The Exercise

Try a physical version of this backwards technique.

Find a seat on a train that faces the opposite direction to which you are travelling.

Let your mind go blank, not worrying about the future, but focusing exactly on where you are now.

Think about what you are leaving behind.

As you depart, write in your notepad. Not in complete sentences, but in fragments, each a quick sketch of the scenery as it passes by.

If necessary, say it out loud and then write it down.

(Don't worry, no one is listening.)

Top Tip

The 'backwards technique' can also be applied to a group setting.

Place some chairs in a circle and turn them away from the centre, so that their backs face the middle of the room.

Sit everyone down, facing away from each other, so no one can see anyone else's face.

When brainstorming ideas, shout out your thoughts, one word a time, so no one is clear who is speaking or which direction the next idea is coming from. Let one person scribe the text, paying particular attention to any elisions or confusions that occur.

These collisions might reveal a new concept, a sudden thought, an idea that belongs collectively to everyone.

Integrate
backwards
working to
change the
future.

16 | RENAME THINGS

- Give the object another name.

- Change its content into something new.

- Alter your own reality with this simple, effective technique.

RENAME THINGS

I like renaming things – I've been doing this all my life.

It's a kind of magic.

Because when you put a new sobriquet on an existing object, you twist the sense of it, push it into another dimension.

So when we rename things, we turn them upside down, making them impregnable, heroic.

The surface of things is mutable, so we can affect our own reality by changing that skin. These bumps, these alterations are like skirmishes on the surface, small dents in reality, where we can change forms, mutate objects and transform our own creativity.

Within these simple games there is a ferocious amount of power, because it needs audacity to rename an object as something else.

For example, I recently saw in a gallery in Nîmes a work by artist Dieter Roth, where he had named an obverse collection of printed items as 'Snow', thus adding an oblique angle on the found material.

I still find this an indubitably radical act, a statement that anything is everything else; the upside down as legitimate as the right way up.

On a more prosaic note, 'renaming exercises' can be very useful in brainstorming situations.

For example, if you are branding a new type of coffee, you might rename it as –

- Claw.
- Unawakened.
- Sioux.
- Misty.
- Intangible.
- Serrated.
- Mood.

All the suggestions on the list above I selected at random from a physical dictionary (always use a real-life version, rather than a virtual one).

Open the page, using the technique on Page 122, and choose one word, if necessary forcing a connection.

Once you have a list, play with the items, sticking the random words together – like 'Unawakened Sioux' or 'Intangible Serrated'.

You might not obtain an immediate name for your product; however, you will have a new window on the process. You can subsequently explore the qualities of this new coffee by using the suggestions hinted at by these unconscious pairings.

What are the feelings inherent in 'Unawakened Sioux'?

Thus a creative ideas session might involve multiple techniques from this book – the 'random book technique' alongside 'read down the page'.

Mix up all these elements.

Top Tip

If you get stuck, integrate OuLiPo's (Ouvroir de Littérature Potentielle) 'S+7' method by using a simple technique.

Take a dictionary and replace any nouns in your text by the same words but seven nouns forward in the book.

In this way finding a completely new meaning.

When we rename things, we turn them upside down, making them impregnable, heroic.

ENDUCTION

Objects can fill us with hope.

They offer solutions outside ourselves.

These objects can be rubbish, things that we find on the street or buy for a few pence – discarded and recycled elements.

We just need to explore these pieces in inventive ways, always interrogating their possibilities.

You have already looked at some of these methods: 'Use Your Hands', 'Follow The Street', 'Be Physical', 'Integrate The Reverse', 'Work Backwards'.

However, ultimately, the revolution in creative thinking lies in your head – inside you.

Your own body is the ultimate object solution.

As a creative leader, you need to be prepared to lead your meeting from the front, with a strong, imaginative direction.

Try everything yourself first.

Open yourself up to process – showing all around you that you are free and unafraid.

The revolution
in creative
thinking lies
in your head.

PROCESS

WORKING WITH PROCESS

This section is about working with process.

Process is the aware part of yourself.

However, rather than individual pinpricks of awareness, isolated in their own singularity, process strings these together in a chain, always making patterns and developing forms.

So you can clearly see what's going on.

If you can observe the pattern, you can have clarity about your own material and can therefore transmit your creative ideas articulately to your team.

The principle of working with these elements is to take you right to the edges of your ability, where all the best ideas lie.

I am interested in framing this creative work against the backdrop of your unconscious, the Wild West, this untamed country of the mind.

Approach the contents of this section with an attitude that's playful and curious – if you do this you won't go far wrong.

All of this can be accomplished by working with process.

At the edges
of your ability,
that's where
all the best
ideas lie.

17

APPLY YOUR INSTINCT

- Use what's in front of you.

- The solution is always within your field of vision.

- Find an answer by moving the parts around as if in a game.

APPLY YOUR INSTINCT

Usually, when I'm working with clients, I ask no questions in advance, nor ask them to prepare any material.

Instead, I might tune in to the first thing that they say when they arrive –

- 'Sorry that I'm late.'
- 'I hope I'm not going to waste your time.'
- 'My first language is not English.'
- 'Do you have a pen?'

Everything can be sensed, in that first statement, in capsule form.

Likewise, sometimes, I believe it's often better not to study the brief in advance, but simply to respond instinctively to the situation, working with your first impulses.

However, this spontaneity is often mediated against in the office environment. The teams want to seal creativity, force it into a series of principles, to make it safe, hermetic and taut.

So creativity meetings usually go on for too long (and are often not about creativity at all, but the team's internal dynamics).

Instead, zigzag to keep the process moving, dynamic.

Top Tip

Brainstorming doesn't have to only happen in group meetings.

Try this –

Take an A4 piece of paper, then walk around the office, stopping at each desk.

Ask for an idea from each person, write it down, then fold over that part of the paper to hide their response.

Continue until the page is folded like a concertina.

At the end, unravel the paper and reveal the jagged narrative. Can any part of the text be used to solve the organisation's current challenges?

Remember, brainstorms can be –

- Five minutes long.
- Images.
- Physical.
- Chains of events.
- Walks.
- On the wall.
- Improvised games.
- Colour swatches.
- Bus rides.
- Objects.

What are 'walks on the wall'?

It's often better not to study the brief in advance, but simply to respond instinctively to the situation.

18 FIND DOUBLE MEANINGS

- Play with the different levels within your text.

- Don't take the words that you see at face value.

- There is an alternative reading that can be found hidden away from view.

FIND DOUBLE MEANINGS

It's important to recognise the power of process.

This kind of interior work might be difficult to justify in a fast-moving work environment. However, the quiet time of self-reflection is necessary to generate interesting, new ideas.

Remember, process is often right in front of your eyes, if you are willing to pay attention, but sometimes you will need to sit with ambiguity to get the best results.

Try it like this –

The Exercise

Look out for any words in your texts or conversations that might have a double meaning.

Like –

- Balance.
- Play.
- Delivery.
- Branch.

These nouns can be reinterpreted as active commands or instructions.

For example, if the word 'balance' emerges (in relation to your finances), then act out this term, playing on its double meaning, by balancing something on your head or your finger.

Let everyone in the group stand up and try out the technique.

In this physically charged improvisation, of balancing, see if you can come up with some further ideas about balancing the company's books.

Similarly, if the word is 'branch', I might free-associate around the word. Branch, twig, leaf. Are there any current problems with the company's 'branches'?

Top Tip
In one group session that I facilitated, the image of a motorcycle delivery man appeared.

Therefore, I was curious to see if the 'delivery' part of the company's service needed some attention. Or even how processes and ideas were 'delivered' internally within the office.

What was accidentally revealed through a throw-away word was, in fact, a useful piece of process for the organisation, highlighting an area of practice that could be worked on, to the advantage of the whole group.

Sit with ambiguity to get the best results.

LATOA

This next exercise extends the process idea into an external methodology.

The Exercise

Line up a product that you are working with.

Set the following instruction: (L) look (A) at (T) the (O) object (A) as –

- Pure shape.
- Where it was made.
- Colour.
- Upside down.
- Association.
- Nature connection.
- Word game.
- Taste.

Rename the item, using three suggestions from each of your team, and attach your new sobriquets on to the object with sticky notes, so that the product becomes covered with new ideas.

Make at least one totally off-the-wall suggestion per item.

(This action is performative, changing the surface of the product and transforming its appearance.)

When I try this exercise myself, I place an empty
bottle on my desk. Using the LATOA instruction
template above, I come up with –

- Neck.
- France.
- Bottle green.
- Red message.
- Desert island.
- Green leaf.
- Leak.
- Corky.

My work is now to jigsaw these texts, to paste and cut,
in the service of a new discovery, a possible output.

If you try this exercise with your team, you will have
many potential suggestions. Be prepared to keep the
exercise mobile, active, fluid – not necessarily output-
focused.

These games of personal process offer you the
possibility of change. So don't shut the door on the
experiment too soon, before anything genuinely
exploratory can happen.

Work with not-knowing.

Frame it as a game, a warm-up, fun, thereby lowering
the stakes.

Top Tip
After several sessions of process, give your team
members handwritten badges with their process-based
associations written on them, characteristics
developed over the sessions, that the team might
call on for help.

Here are some of my suggestions –

- Ask me.
- I give a useful overview.
- Chance card.
- I am a willing participant.
- Shuffle.
- Visual expert.
- I am good at taking risks.

In this way you move towards developing your own
system of creative cards (like my '210CARDS'), an
instruction deck that you can search through each
time you want to articulate your process.

This is the beginning of liberation.

Note how I created the name LATOA, on Page 168,
using a simple acrostic.

LATOA reminds me of an island in the Pacific and so
with this image in place, my process work can sit
here, physically on this rocky outcrop, like a reminder
of an interior idea – exotic, dangerous, fertile.

Don't shut the door on the experiment too soon, before anything genuinely exploratory can happen.

19

MAKE A PACK OF CARDS

- Develop your own pack of cards.

- So you can shuffle your thoughts.

- Every time you want a solution, pick a card from the deck.

MAKE A PACK OF CARDS

Many people have used cards as a way to channel and direct their own process –

- *I Ching*.
- George Brecht's 'Water Yam'.
- Tarot cards.
- Brian Eno and Peter Schmidt's 'Oblique Strategies'.
- Edward de Bono's 'Think Links'.

Sometimes people use these systems for telling the future, but I prefer to use them to find out about now (a more tricky proposition).

Don't reply to the standard coaching question and think about what you will be doing in five years' time; instead focus on what you are doing now, in the next five minutes.

Who are you right now?

Use card packs to direct you there.

The Exercise

Make a small card deck that you regularly use to check in on your own creativity.

Write a series of ten cards with simple instructions on them.

Like –

- Back to front.
- Image bank.
- Peripheral thoughts.
- Use the obvious.
- Explore conflict.
- Find a bigger space.
- Instinctive approach.
- Colour strategies.
- Multiple viewpoints.
- Keep it small.

(Choose your own instructions.)

The packs can be as hard-edged or as amorphous as you like, depending on the needs of the business, with many open-ended instructions, suitable for interpretation.

Each time that you face a creative impasse, shuffle the pack, choose a card and follow its instruction.

Keep the cards on your desk and refer to them regularly. Your own pack should be used in a very active manner, giving direction when needed in a purposeful and dynamic way.

This adds a density to your practice, a complexity that is enviable, decisive.

You will find that even after a few days, something will shift, rub off, and you will become more tuned in to your own creativity.

Slowly build up more items in the pack, until you have a larger selection of statements.

Continue to add to this process, augmenting your own physical toolkit of processes that you can use in creative sessions. This might take several weeks and could include many cards.

Top Tip
If you are working in a team and you notice that your sessions often evoke repeated ideas, think about formalising these thoughts into a set of actions.

Write these words on to individual index cards.

Your ten actions might be –

- Output.
- Team.
- Generate.
- Backwards.
- Customer.
- Stop.
- Retail.
- Start again.
- Creative.
- Flip.

Shuffle the pack to ascertain your current area of focus.

I recently worked with a photographer on a set of these action cards – when he was stuck or nervous on a shoot, he selected a card from the pack to remind himself of what he should be doing.

Bringing him back to himself.

Write a series of ten cards with simple instructions on them.

SHUFFLE THE GROUP

I call this exercise 'shuffle the group' as it challenges everyone in the team to be a leader, each person participating fully in the session.

Try it this way –

The Exercise

Think about the skills that might be exhibited by your team. For example, perhaps some people are good at –

- Ideas.
- Images.
- Feedback.
- Details.
- Slogans.
- Outputs.

Create your own skills catalogue, an inventory of all the abilities present in the group. Write these qualities on individual index cards.

In meetings, let each person select at random one of the cards.

Even if they choose a skill where they don't have expertise, allow them to try that, for the duration of the session. So, for example, someone who isn't used to working with images might pick that card and have to attempt it, to the best of their ability.

Thus you don't only shuffle the cards, you shuffle the group.

This is the complete opposite of what usually happens in business. Normally, you recognise a skill, an ability, and hold on to it, whatever else happens. However, this can sometimes become a barrier to change. It's this fixity that is the curse of creativity – the set routine, the known formula.

Most of the time, use your normal exercises, then occasionally run a 'shuffle the group' session and quite unexpectedly force your team members to change roles. Or use the method for ten minutes at the end of a meeting, to undermine rigid solutions.

Top Tip
In your group, in the first two minutes, if you notice that your team is sitting in their usual chairs, instruct them to take a new place next to someone with whom they don't often work.

Even better, take the chairs and tables out of the room and encourage them to stand, floating in a kind of unconscious soup, ready to move physically close to the good idea when it emerges.

When they feel inspired by something that they hear, ask them to cluster around the person who proposed it.

Keep the action alive.

It's not about winning approval but about loosening the cultural bonds that attach us so easily to habitual processes.

Keep the physical demands moving, even if only for one minute.

Keep the physical demands moving, even if only for one minute.

20

CREATE CONFLICT

- Don't fear difficult feelings.

- Approach them with an open mind.

- Use the dynamics of the group to explore your current challenges.

CREATE CONFLICT

In this rush of exercises and techniques, don't forget the quiet voice of one who doesn't go with the flow.

(I never wanted to go with the flow.)

So be careful of the need to supply fast, glib solutions to difficult client briefs.

Be the person who sometimes has to say 'Stop'.

The answer is always underneath, in between, overturned.

To do this you must ask some very basic questions –

- Who am I?
- Where am I?
- What can I see?
- What's in front of me?
- What am I doing?
- Where am I going?
- What's inside?

Don't forget the authenticity of your approach, your experience, your process.

This might be difficult, as it could create conflict.

However, conflict is an essential part of creative development.

For example, this recently happened to me in a workshop setting.

One group member brought in a 1p coin, as her found item, because she liked the colour. However, the penny had an explosive effect; the team found it challenging to try to integrate this element into their work.

It brought up the core issue of money in a very direct manner.

In creative work we often push difficulty away; however, the problematic is always the best territory to investigate for new ideas, so don't be afraid if things don't work out as planned.

On another occasion, when I ran this exercise in a workshop, one of the group kicked over a very ordered construction by another participant. I stepped back, as it was the group's responsibility to process the conflict. Yet there was nothing wrong with this impulse. It was a legitimate part of the creative cycle.

In our adult lives we become very adept at avoiding the problem and side-stepping conflict, going with the consensus in creative meetings. Process allows us to be more direct, less mediated, more playful, full of our actual feelings about things.

Therefore I like the word 'process' because it's a very provocative concept and likely to change the dynamics of a situation.

The answer
is always
underneath,
in between,
overturned.

21 | INTEGRATE FEELINGS

- Integrate the 90% that you don't normally use.

- Put the feelings on the table.

- Explore life at the edges of what is known.

INTEGRATE FEELINGS

Process = feelings.

When developing creative ideas, we are always exploring our emotions. We pretend that the work is about the product, the team, the client or the brand.

But it's always about feelings.

These are like a hidden iceberg, occupying 90% of the space in meetings, but entirely invisible.

If you are working in a creative team, whether you realise it or not, you might spend a lot of time holding these feelings at bay.

In fact, I have been in meetings and workshops where the entire proceedings are about trying to suppress any emotional response from the group.

Yet, paradoxically, the products and processes that you are attempting to sell to others, to consumers, are all about emotional engagement.

Therefore the answers to any creative problem are always about the feelings.

Likewise, your own small exposure, your own embarrassment, can often be useful in processing your creativity.

It reveals that you are at the edge of what is possible (personally or professionally), facing a wall.

You understand what you can and what you can't do.

You are preparing to leap into new territory.

If you find that –

- Your ears burn.
- Your palms are sweaty.
- Your throat dries up.
- Your head feels hot.

Recognise that something important is happening.

Slow down and feel the embarrassment.

Sometimes I even draw attention to it, saying 'That's interesting. I'm suddenly getting hot. I wonder what's going on?' Instead of denying it, which makes the feeling worse, I build an immediate dialogue with my fear.

I use it as good information.

If I have a problem with public speaking, when facing a large audience, I always use this technique to settle myself on stage. It works because it shows my vulnerability, the degree of humility.

An admittance that not everything always goes right.

Top Tip

If you are a creative leader, always make sure that the exposure you evoke in your team is not shaming.

Include an invitation at the start of each session, making it clear that participation is voluntary.

Embarrassment only works if it's good-natured and playful.

Be cautious of provocation.

Embarrassment is the fuzzy outline around each of us, a place where our inner core mixes with the social space of perception and doubt.

Ideas can often be found in this area of blurriness.

However, probe slowly.

Ask open questions, designed to set the person free, rather than close down to fear.

Always allow an exit.

Slow down
and feel the
embarrassment.

WATER AND SAND

Process directs you back to your first experiences of play, as a child, when you put contradictory things together, working in exploratory ways.

In my process philosophy, I'm using exercises that evoke these early childhood experiences to challenge the boundaries between physical things, forcing the client to think again.

Water and sand – can these elements not go together?

When we were young, we chose games that perfectly suited our environment.

We didn't think about creativity, we just did it. We were alive, uncontained.

Therefore, decades later, encouraged to look again at play, we can often find useful ways of integrating this elemental exuberance into our current working lives.

For example, as a child –

- Did you rely on cooperation?
- Did you build spaces?
- Did you thrive on challenge?
- Did you connect with objects?
- Did you work in a team?
- Did you investigate risk?
- Did you focus on feelings?

If so, try to integrate some of these approaches into the office environment –

- Add drawings to the walls.
- Create a two-person ideas tent.
- Place a bunk bed in the office, for dream space.
- Build a materials corner, full of cardboard and foil.
- Colour-code pathways through the desks.
- Use a goal net for concept football.

And if this means playing five-a-side with your team, visiting the woods, building a den with staff members, then don't be afraid to try it.

These play encounters test us to drop our adult mask of cool irony and adopt a more flexible attitude, each idea built on spontaneity, decisiveness and chance.

Top Tip
I believe in process methodology – the day-by-day integration of the accidental, in profound ways, through the application of awareness.

This ethos often has tangible business results – your team suddenly gets an opportunity to play with materials in a new and unrestricted way.

They forget the computer for a day and work with objects instead.

What emerges is fluid, unformed, flexible, plastic.

People
Like
Always
Your

Generosity
And
Magnanimity
Every
Second

Ideas are built
on spontaneity,
decisiveness
and chance.

22 | TRUST WHAT YOU CAN'T SEE

- Trust what you can't see in front of you.

- However oblique it might appear to others.

- Integrate the maverick to explore these new areas of the imagination.

TRUST WHAT YOU CAN'T SEE

As you step into the unconscious, as if through a
window, you become a different version of yourself.

You are an astronaut, you are a child.

(No, really.)

You return to play.

One of the exercises that I use with groups is a simple
two-minute technique to help them focus. I ask them
to direct their attention to what they can see right in
front of them.

However, when I time the exercise with a stopwatch,
I deliberately give them longer, so that by the end they
are struggling to find something to describe.

In these unclouded, primitive moments, strange things
start to happen.

1-2-3-4 minutes.

They dig deep into themselves and the images that
they find are exotic, peculiar, quite beyond cliché –
giant blue birds, pink pop-up shops, trees that speak.

Repeated on the page they sound odd, irrational,
occurring as they do on the fringes of consciousness,
far from the logical mind.

Yet, in each instance, they move things forward for the person who activated the image.

So remember, it's useful to push yourself.

Take a bit of extra time to search beyond the obvious.

- Work live.
- Trust what you can't see.
- Accept intuition.
- Use what's in the room.

My techniques are maverick. They often turn things upside down, or reveal answers that you don't expect.

If you use these methods, you will be working with elements that are not obvious, logical or solid.

This can be very challenging.

Yet, if you only want to work with creative ideas from a place of safety, very little can be achieved. Or the concepts, if they emerge, will often be formulaic.

The Exercise

Whatever remains invisible, record that.

Integrate the things that you would normally reject.

Live on the fringes of perception, stay there for a minute and then return with what you have found.

Whatever
remains
invisible,
record that.

FRINGES OF PERCEPTION

Here is a another technique that is very useful for
stimulating ideas.

Try it this way –

The Exercise

Take five minutes to look out of a window.

Remain focused. What attracts your attention?

Once you find something, zoom in on it. It doesn't
matter what the item is, or whether it seems
important, keep focusing your attention on the object.

Write down your observations.

Then try something else. Look straight ahead but
zoom right out, beyond the frame of the window. What
do you see now? Even if the resulting images become
abstract, still record them in your notepad.

Briefly process your results. Where did your eye direct
you? Don't worry if these elements are fantasy items,
aliens, volcanoes, lights – try and integrate them into
your ongoing creative work.

Everything that you see, in or out of this frame, is you.
So if you see a volcano, you know that something is
going to erupt soon.

Thus, material on the fringes can provide you with a good source of creative input, both images and concepts.

However, if you don't have five minutes to look out of a window, if you are in a meeting, just draw a frame on your notepad page and repeat the exercise.

Like this –

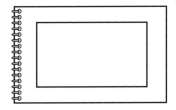

What do you see?

The drawing of the frame pushes your thoughts towards new ideas by dictating the exact conditions where they might arise.

It provides a limit.

In or outside the window, all is possible. You simply project your question into an imaginary frame.

Ideas have nothing to do with received notions of 'inspiration', but rather they emerge by creating artificial devices (a frame, a game, a limit) that force you towards the edges of process, revealing the more oblique elements of your unconscious.

In this instance, the window frame is your frame of reference.

Top Tip
My creativity is not an open space; it's more of a machine where I go every day to find material.

I keep going until I find something that I like.

Creativity is the thinking factory.

Project your question into an imaginary frame.

23

EVOKE DREAM ANALYSIS

- Play with toys.

- Use them as ciphers.

- Build a dialogue with your creative self through the activity of this metaphorical world.

EVOKE DREAM ANALYSIS

Recently, I was looking at some photos of Sigmund Freud's consulting room at the Freud Museum when I noticed that the surface of his desk was covered by many small figures from the ancient world.

These objects were talismanic presences that SF could draw on, a residue of his own internal process.

However, you don't need to be Dr Freud to use these objects. You can try the technique in a much less psychoanalytic form, whilst having similar results.

Try it this way –

The Exercise

Buy some cheap second-hand toys, miniatures, of all sorts.

I see these at car boot sales, or in charity shops, always loaded into a square biscuit tin. They are usually available for a few pennies each.

Choose –

- Cartoon characters.
- Monsters.
- Robots.
- Colourful animals.
- Dinosaurs.

Don't think too much about your selection. Buy them quickly, without really looking too closely at what they represent. If possible, purchase in bulk.

When you are stuck, pull out at random two of the objects, then encourage them to begin a dialogue – the dinosaur with the wicked witch, the silver robot with the jousting knight, the chicken with the cosy cottage.

Use their qualities to debate any of your current challenges. For example, use the chicken to peck holes in any argument that the cosy cottage might generate.

These inanimate figures can be used in exactly the same way that Freud manipulated his ancient objects, to illuminate and penetrate current problems.

In fact, the free gifts at fast-food restaurants, tie-ins from cartoons, whilst not having the profundity of the ancient pantheon, often embody similar qualities: bravery, fear, doubt.

Use the chicken, the robot, the cottage, to answer any queries you might have.

- Who can you find to help you?
- How do you cut through problems?
- How can the toys intervene?
- Can you invite magic to appear?

Thus these talismanic objects become items of psychic ventriloquism, useful for penetrating problems in inquisitive and interesting ways.

Of course, if you are going, even in some small way, to follow the path of Sigmund Freud, the process might be exposing, tough, rigorous and embarrassing.

Even foolish things can push you through the frontiers of creativity. Even the chicken, if given the right problem to work on, can offer a just solution.

If necessary seek professional help to process more complex images. Lie on the couch and allow them to untangle the dream process.

In this floating state, back reclined, the clouds of meaning can be debated by genuine Freudian analysis.

Even foolish things can push you through the frontiers of creativity.

24 | USE MAGIC

- Collect magic objects.

- Support yourself by amassing appurtenances that you can draw on for inspiration.

- The more you use them, the more their magic will rub off on you.

USE MAGIC

Within my methods I'm consciously evoking the research of Lucien Lévy-Bruhl, particularly his book 'The 'Soul' Of The Primitive', a volume of surprising pieces of information about tribal magic.

LLB had an influence on the work of C.G. Jung and his ideas about the collective unconscious.

However, where Lévy-Bruhl is really useful is his collection of anthropological stories about very diverse tribal practices using objects – bees, rocks, trees, animals – and the complex ways human beings relate to these items.

In the modern Western world, particularly in the area of business, we might regard some of these practices as bogus, supernatural and illogical.

A kind of hocus-pocus.

Some might consider this material as mere magical practice, the lowest level of human psychic development. However, for this very reason, I find the relationship to objects, described by Lévy-Bruhl, to be very useful – they are outside our normal range of reference and so catapult us back to our own 'primitive' mind, a place where we are personally unprotected, not immured by habit.

And, for a brief second, when these defences come down, we can become open to new ideas.

The Exercise

Keep a box of tools on your desk, a selection of process items that you find useful – cards, notepad, pencil, cut-up scissors (we have already covered these objects in the book).

Put them in a clearly defined area, with a line around, to indicate their potential. Allow yourself to be the only person to use them.

Whenever you need a new idea, bring out these special materials.

Take five minutes away from your desk, in the canteen, or on the street, and use one of these processes to further an idea –

- Cut-ups.
- Rubbish.
- Word associations.
- The street.
- Folds.

Try 'street folds'.

Don't be ashamed of integrating these techniques. If someone notices you, treat it as if it were a performance, a heightened experience.

This will add to the magical quality.

Of course, visibility is its own challenge.

However, if you take the philosophy of this section to heart – that habit often places a wall between you and the creative idea; that magic can release you from the bonds that tie you down – then treat this enhanced visibility as a chance to fly.

Cautiously, carefully navigate the space.

The walls of the world can dissolve (if you want them to).

Objects

catapult us back to our own 'primitive' mind, a place where we are personally unprotected and not immured by habit.

APPURTENANCES

In the business world, you might often be asked to present new ideas rapidly, after a quick turnaround.

Over many months, this often leaves you with very shallow resources; you might feel exposed, on the spot – with few support structures to draw on.

Working with objects, whether notepads, cards or instruction sets, allows you to build up personal resources that are quite rich in their complexity.

They can't be diminished, because they draw on something deep in you, something that has evolved over time.

Therefore, it's useful to amass objects and processes that give you this stockpile of ideas. When you are stuck, turn to objects – to see what's there, inside yourself.

Appurtenances are personal items, things that you touch that retain something of your personality –

- Coins.
- Watches.
- Spectacles.
- Cigarettes.
- Buttons.

Many of the items that I use for generating ideas
I have collected over a number of years.

For example, a set of counters that I use in my
workshops to determine colour – they are actually
plastic bus tokens – were bought from a market stall
in Rio de Janeiro.

I remember walking down the street with artist Nathan
Gray, coming out of the underground, discussing the
potential of these hexagons (NG 'It's the magic shape.').

As I read my diaries from this time in Brazil,
recollecting this event, the feeling floods back and
it's this exact quality of magic that is contained in
the simple coloured discs.

Something comes from my hands into the object,
an accumulation of self, of essence, that is useful
in conjuring up ideas.

The *I Ching* has a resonance for me, as a tool, for
similar reasons. The book was generated by many
people, over a long period, and so has the feeling
of several hands, multiple voices.

However, everyone has this human magic in their
fingertips, in their touch.

The Exercise

Collect and integrate personal objects. Use them in simple, effective ways, acting out their qualities in a physical manner.

- Flip a chosen coin to make decisions.
- Hold your spectacles at arm's length to really see the client brief, optically charged.
- Spin a button and before it lands, force yourself to have an idea.

Your will is always activated by these alternative methods, allowing you to step into the unknown, the unpredictable energy of the active present.

Top Tip
Here's another twist on this same idea –

I once had a client who turned up ten minutes late for an appointment. So, instead of forgetting about these lost minutes, I asked him to take his own watch and turn back time, rewinding ten minutes into the past. Now, in this magic space generously given to him, he could think about what he really wanted.

- What did he mean to say?
- What did he think he was avoiding?
- What did he want to do?

If time was reversed for a moment, what could really happen?

Step into the unknown, the unpredictable energy of the active present.

BETTER MAGIC

Recently I've been activating my creative potential by doing something incredible; I have been looking at things.

I have been paying attention.

Whether it's a plate on the table, a train, a pattern of clouds or mud in the gutter – I have been looking directly at things.

I thought that I already did this, but I realised that I never really saw or paid attention to anything around me.

So my world slid by.

When I started doing this simple exercise, for a few seconds each day, I understood that I felt happy, alive, content to be myself.

I created a magic zone.

Of course, nothing can mitigate against the hardship of the world, with all its challenges.

Yet these split seconds of happiness helped me.

If being alive means anything (I'm not sure if it does) then it must mean BEING ALIVE, noticing everything that comes in through the eyes, the hands, the skin.

To deny this is to be uncreative.

To deny this is to avoid life.

Because when you activate creativity, when you become the best version of yourself, when you excel, when you transcend your limitations, you approach life in a direct way.

That is the 'Better Magic' of this book – the day to day, the ordinary world finally revealed.

Many names have been attached to this 'magic' over the ages; some call it 'unconscious', some 'awareness' or some even 'imagination' but I believe it's really human potential working at its best to manifest something incredible.

You are incredible.

You carry this unconscious potential with you every minute of every day, in your head, ready to be activated.

You need nothing other than yourself.

If you take one thing away from reading this book, remember that you are creative, you are alive and you are incredible.

You are
incredible.

ENDUCTION

You already knew the content of this book, more or less, even before you read it.

Why?

Because inside you there is a huge library of information, the unconscious, ready to solve even the most intractable creative problems.

If you can trust in your own intuition.

Believe in the ready-made solutions that sit inside of you, in order to move dynamically ahead.

Use the techniques that you have learned in this part of the book: 'Apply Your Instinct', 'Make A Pack Of Cards', 'Trust What You Can't See', 'Integrate Feelings', 'Use Magic'.

This journey is not easy. But with perseverance, tenacity and kindness, it's possible to advance.

Creativity = the self.

So enlarge yourself as the best preparation for having original ideas. Difference is where new things emerge.

Remain aware and something is certain to shift.

Remain aware and something is certain to shift.

MICHAEL ATAVAR

Michael Atavar is an artist and a creative consultant with a practice that mixes creativity, business, art and psychology.

He works with individuals and businesses, helping to solve professional problems, using creativity as a key.

www.creativepractice.com

ACKNOWLEDGEMENTS

Many thanks for advice and support to Roelof Bakker, Martin Crawley, Robert Cuming, Nathan Gray, Miles Hanson, Birgit Heinisch, Steven Whinnery, Pat Winfield.

Illustrations by Richard Scarborough.

Thanks to Què és.

Many thanks to Tate Modern Public Programmes for providing the resources for 'Flatford Mill (Scene On A Navigable River)'.

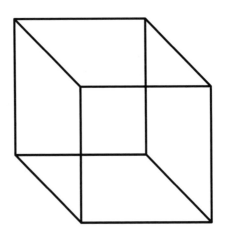

NOTES ON THE CREATIVE UNCONSCIOUS

In this book the 'unconscious' is used to mean that which is not immediately present in the real world.

What sits under the surface of the mind.

It's not used in a technical sense (does it even really exist?) but, rather, to define a space of the imagination – the continual volume of sense impressions that you carry with you day and night.

In this book I call this material the 'creative unconscious' (as a small echo of Freud, Jung, Neumann etc.).

The unconscious can be unpredictable. In group contexts it provokes strong feelings. Proceed at your own pace, finding your way. However, if you want to work more fully in this area of the mind, you might consider taking on further training or working with an experienced supervisor.

Do not take personal risks. If in doubt, don't do it. Reconsider and wait for another opportunity when you have more resources to address the situation.

Never work at the edge of your limits. Always take a step back.

The unconscious is yours alone. Do not act out the material in real life and never involve other people in these interior narratives.

Take time to process the results of teamwork and avoid any hasty judgements.

If you are engaged with groups, select rooms where the doors can be closed, providing a useful protection between the exploratory unconscious of inside and the everyday material of outside.

Use these boundaries to build a strong container for your creative work.

Always make the limits solid and definite –

- Adhere to exact start times.
- Ensure commitment from the group.
- Put your feet on the ground.

Keep caution uppermost in your mind.

The more that you work with the unconscious, the more safety you will need to integrate. Often this feels like a constant rebuilding of boundaries, day by day, to protect the soft core that gets revealed through process. However, in time, these simple procedures will become easier to incorporate.

Whether it exists or not, whether you believe in it or not, whether you feel that you possess it or not, you can use the creative unconscious to enrich your working life.

In this sense the 'unconscious' is always real.

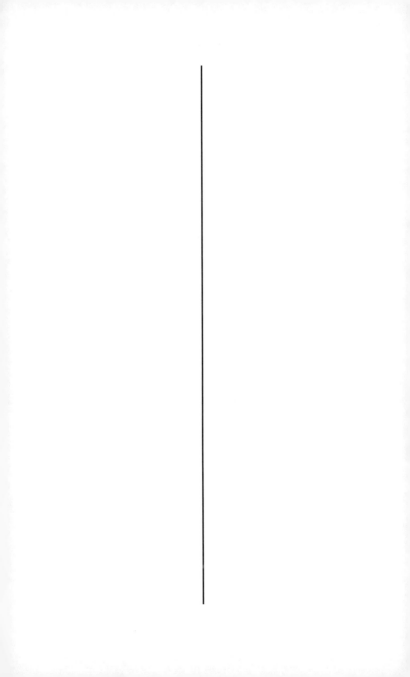